Oriental Poetry

Toward the Sun

2022

Oriental Poetry

Toward the Sun

2022

Yellow Moon Poets

Oriental Poetry
Toward the Sun
2022
Paperback

ISBN: 978-1-943974-87-0

Published by;
Shoestring Book Publishing.
Maine, USA

Copyright © 2022 By, Yellow Moon Poets
Edited by, Diane Allen Hemingway
Cover Artist: Diane Allen Hemingway, "Corners"
All rights reserved.
Printed in the United States of America.

No part of this book may be reproduced, stored in a retrieval system, or transmitted in any form, electronic, mechanical; or by other means whatsoever, without written permission from the author. Except for the case of brief quotations within reviews and critical articles.

Layout and design by Shoestring Book Publishing

For information address;
shoestringpublishing4u@gmail.com
www.shoestringbookpublishing.com

Foreword

When people gather together, united in a common interest, they form a community. And that is what we have on Allpoetry.com- a corner, within that poetic universe, of an enthusiastic, talented, supportive group of poets deeply in love with the Oriental poetic forms. The Yellow Moon Poets, or the Moonies, as we affectionately call ourselves represent all the continents (except, possibly Antarctica, but who really knows if there is a penguin masquerading as a poet amongst us...). We write the well-known Japanese poetic forms of haiku, tanka, haibun, tanka prose, sedoka etc. We dabble in that most beloved of Arabic/Urdu/Persian forms, the ghazal, and we do it in English. We have tried our hands at other lesser known forms such as the Sijo from Korea; the Pathya Vat from Thailand, the Cherita from Malaysia and the Ya du from Burma/Myanmar. We write solo, and we have collaborated. Many of our poets have taken the excellent, free classes in haiku and tanka writing offered on the site. We are very proud of our many poets who have published in mainstream haiku and tanka publications and won awards in various international contests.

Our isolation was lessened in these past two years because we had the group to hang out with, virtually, to be inspired to write, often in response to the many prompts in contests hosted by members. Isolation also brought about the need, and ability to focus on the moment, look within, suspend judgements and appreciate life. We hope you will find and enjoy glimmers of these themes throughout this book.

Suraja M Roychowdhury

Table of contents

Foreword - Suraja M Roychowdhury vii
Preface Colleen - Selvon-Rampersad xii
    Mary Lou and Paul 1
Mary Lou and Paul - Colleen Selvon-Rampersad 3
Harmer B. 'Bud' Cole, Jr. 1942 - 2022 4
Mary Lou Healy - April 26, 1927 - August 6, 2021 5
  Paul J. Geiger January 12, 1930 - August 9, 2021 12
  Harmer B. 'Bud' Cole, Jr 1942 - 2022. 19
    Spring 25
By the light of eos – Ghazal, Madhu Singh 27
  Srinivasa Rao Sambangi 28
  Maureen Edden 29
  Ixxehi Destiny Izehi 30
  Michael Morris 31
  Diane Allen Hemingway 32
  Gina 33
  Claire Rosilda 34
  Colleen Selvon-Rampersad aka cosera 35
  Suraja Roychowdhury 36
  Lux 37
  Ron Russell 38
spring in the city - Orense Nicod 39
    Summer 41
  Kanjini Devi 43

Orense Nicod 44
Suraja Roychowdhury 45
Ixxehi Destiny Izehi 46
Diane Allen Hemingway 47
Srinivasa Rao Sambangi 48
Madhu Singh 49
Ron Russell 50
Michael Morris 51
Kanjini Devi 52
Claire Rosilda 53
Marlene E. Kasahara 54
Sue Colpitts 55
Maureen Edden 56

Heart to Heart - Colleen Selvon-Rampersad aka cosera 57
   haibun / haiku ....
   Lux 58
      Autumn 59
   Maureen Edden 61
   Srinivasa Rao Sambangi 62
   Colleen Selvon-Rampersad aka cosera 63
   Kathryne Ankney Higheagle 64
   Kanjini Devi 65
   Madhu Singh 66
   Sue Colpitts, Sijo 67
   Sijo 67

shinrin- yoku (forest bathing) - Anton R. Kelian & Sue Colpitts 68

   Orense Nicod 69

half the moon - Suraja Roychowdhury, Ghazal 70

   Diane Allen Hemingway 71

   Ron Russell 72

   Gina 73

   Michael Morris 74

   chick-a-dee Rengay Kathryne Ankney Higheagle and James W. McRight Jr. 75

Winter 77

   Claire Rosilda 79

   Kanjini Devi 80

   Sue Colpitts 81

   Anton R. Kelian 82

   Suraja Roychowdhury 83

   Marlene E. Kasahara 84

A wave of winter: 85

   Diane Allen Hemingway 86

   Maureen Edden 87

   Ron Russell 88

   Srinivasa Rao Sambangi 89

   Gina 90

   Madhu Singh 91

   Michael Morris 92

   Colleen Selvon-Rampersad aka cosera 93

Orense Nicod 94
    Lose Yourself, by Eminem 95
Jason Mackey 97
Diane Hines 98
Kathryne Ankney Higheagle 99
Colleen Selvon-Rampersad 100
Maureen Edden 101
Madhu Singh 102
Firdaus Parvez 103
Diane Allen Hemingway 104
Afterword - Diane Allen Hemingway 105

Preface

Who doesn't like a splash of spice? As I recall, variety is the spice of life, and poets prove that saying to be true, as we put pens together to present OP 2022.

Literary strengths emerge after fishing for words in waves of sentiment and surprise, undaunted moods, pain and sadness, adventure and laughter, all in life and death.

Taste the diverse flavours spiced with international contributions. Go ahead, enjoy!

Colleen Selvon-Rampersad

Mary Lou and Paul

Mary Lou and Paul

I was amazed that Paul Geiger was born in 1930.

He was the one always alerting me when I got gold or silver. Always congratulating, whether he copped first or last place. Paul was quick-witted, an eristic Mr Eveready engaging in a friendly argument.

So energetic! Love them dearly.

I recall Mary Lou Healy, almost 94. She was ready to offer a tip, even if it meant that I would be ahead of her in a contest. Sweet, sweet, memories are made of this.

> two dear haijins
> resting on a cloud
> Paul and M'lou
> their tales of the Orient
> linger on our hearts

Colleen Selvon-Rampersad

Harmer B. 'Bud' Cole, Jr. 1942 - 2022

Ah, unforgettable. Bud Cole, he was filled with encouraging remarks and meaningful suggestions. His barking really had no bite. Like Paul Geiger, he was a zesty sparring partner. Bud was generous in commendation when he found pleasure in reading a poem that appealed to him.

Bud Cole's demise may have nipped at our joy but not entirely. His creative penning found a place within our hearts. One of his haiku was chosen by HSA as the best that year in Frogpond. Our love for him lives on.

    Cento: the old river
                with memories of you
                sunset

Colleen Selvon-Rampersad aka cosera

Ladies first:

Mary Lou Healy

April 26, 1927 - August 6, 2021

Hummingbird
beak-deep in delight
honeysuckle

When life quickens and the long dark waiting months vanquish in joy. So it is when life begins. And so it is sometimes, when life moves quietly to its conclusion. This is my month, my debut on earth's stage. I welcome it in gratitude for yet another season, for yet another turning of the sun toward light.

I wait for returned geese to cry out overhead; for robins to appear, their beaks filled with nest building treasure, for the grass to be starred with tiny blossoms. And, I wait for the turning calendar to show April's 26th day, on which, fate being agreeable, I will turn 94.

calendar rustle
numbers fall like spring petals
turning turning

dawn breaks
in the morning glory's eye
a prayer call

I swat
the air around my head
no-see-ums

This night is deep in silence, shrouded in darkness, shadowy forms felt rather than seen.

black cloud
blows away overhead
a second moonrise

fallen fruit
under my apple tree
a munching rabbit

nibble nose
testing the doneness
spitting seeds

a tasty treat
for early summer and
unexpected too

Paul J. Geiger

January 12, 1930 - August 9, 2021

lack of attention
to my garden
California poppies

here children play
within the graves
blooming flowers

blooming poppies
around the graves
children play

just over
the next dune
oasis?

reducing
backyard fire hazard
weed whacker

while you jog notice small things pleasant surprises

abandoned
dairy warehouse
a buttercup field

Harmer B. 'Bud' Cole, Jr.

1942 - 2022

Starbucks —
thoughts
fill the poets cup

and this is why I sojourn here
on the cold hill side
alone and palely loitering
I saw their starved lips in the gloam
and no birds sing

my lips
upon your brow
embers glow
early teens pastime, circa 1950s,
stealing a kiss while seated around a makeshift fire
on the beach of the Delaware river
sipping KoolAid and bragging (lying) about everything ...

mobbed outdoor buffet
birds at the
suet blocks

Spring

By the light of eos

Apple blossoms shimmer by the light of eos
Is the moon their mirror by the light of eos
Is that a goblet of wine or a cupped red rose
As heady however by the light of eos
Lavender orchids cling close to the old oak tree
Its gnarled trunk shines silver by the light of eos
Dewdrops roll off dahlias in the rising mist
As pretty as heather by the light of eos
Daffodils toss their heads in an enchanted dance
Crisply blows the zephyr by the light of eos

Ghazal

Madhu Singh

croaking frog
my love song receives
laughter in splashes

Srinivasa Rao Sambangi

mossy stillness
by the stream's bend
a primrose

Maureen Edden

terracotta blooms
under the brackish tree
flower calabash

skylark's devotion
her whistles wobble into
the sunrise

constellation
of dark green dandelions—
hog plums

unsung sungod
from bamboo's hollow
hunch flautist's
silhouette

midday cockcrow
today's sunrise falls aloof
rain puddle ripples

Ixxehi Destiny Izehi

busy bees
wrens basking in the fragrance
of apple blossom

Michael Morris

pining away
during dreadful times
a robin's nest
on the pine branch
bring spring's pleasant thoughts

Diane Allen Hemingway

a bee hovers
over froth and gossip
coffee morning

Gina

first cuckoo
so much repetition
on the war memorial

Claire Rosilda

sleepless oldster
desperate to swat fly—
baited mouse trap

Colleen Selvon-Rampersad aka cosera

when the wind blows
through holes in the bamboo

does it know

that my heart too was pierced
with the notes of our song

Suraja Roychowdhury

a slow walk around
the same promenade
last spring till now
to all lost smiles
my green bouquet

Lux

kindred spirits
chasing dreams
butterflies

Ron Russell

spring in the city

Spring in the city still comes, even with concrete and stone walling off greater nature views.

In this grey labyrinth I find cherry blossoms and magnolia trees in full bloom. After a few turns, daffodils and tulips sway to breezes sculpted through the city's veins. I feel the surge pushing against the clouds, the breath of spring. Petals drift and branches lift towards the sun.

Foxglove trees line the way back and every late spring afternoon the fragrance of purple crushed on the asphalt leads me home.

apple blossoms
in cobalt reflections
Van Gogh skyscrapers

Orense Nicod

Summer

summer breeze
bows to autumn gust
over sand dunes
where once we were bright eyed
weaving our dreams

Kanjini Devi

solstice sunrise
gilding the green oak
an old druid

Orense Nicod

caviar on toast...
I would much rather watch
the sturgeon moon

Suraja Roychowdhury

croaky choir
setting the night agog
midnight sunrise

early coos
in the morning lawns
due drop of dew

hog plums jackpot
the squirrel whisks away
a nutmeg

evening crows
a cricket mimics
stridulation

Milky Way
fireflies constellate
my bedroom boredom

august visitor
sleeks through staycation window
moonflower whisps

Ixxehi Destiny Izehi

Juneteenth ~
a step into
the solstice

Diane Allen Hemingway

summer afternoon
ice cream street vendor
enjoys the heat

Srinivasa Rao Sambangi

As the sun's charioteer, Arun, reins in his seven white horses, steering them westward, the incandescence of the North Indian summer sky dims.

The crones gather on the raised platform around the neem tree's trunk. They gargle on a hookah, passing it around. Gossip about daughter-in-laws dies down as the subject of discussion brings in tea. A brass tray laden with thick glass tumblers, filled three-fourths with piping hot milky tea.

As they sip the brew, sweat beads on their forehead and upper lip, and then cools them, evaporating in the light breeze fanned up by the abundant tiny neem leaves. After tea, the ladies indulge in another round of the aromatic tobacco blended with jaggery. Then they sing bhajans with gusto, each trying to drown the other's offkey voice.

banyan dusk
the sun dips over
from the crow's claw

Madhu Singh

only ripples
across the surface
the stone sinks

Ron Russell

dance for me
come closer
dragonfly

Michael Morris

all the cows
at standstill facing north
solstice storm

Kanjini Devi

I turn, restless in half-sleep, and feel the tide seeping away. 'Don't go!' I call out.

> no-one's child
> on an empty beach
> crying gulls
> will this feeling
> never leave me
>
> ***Claire Rosilda***

June heatwave
sunshine and bees entangled
in the native oaks

Marlene E. Kasahara

between heaven and earth -
a caterpillar climbs
my arm

entre ciel et terre -
une chenille grimpe
mon bras

Sue Colpitts

deep in the forest
songs of a nightingale
sweet sorrow

Maureen Edden

Heart to Heart

Whenever I rushed home early to complete my husband's unfinished chores, he would pull an Elvis kiss-curl on his forehead and croon, I love you for a hundred thousand reasons...

        I love you for
        a hundred thousand reasons
        music binds us

        music binds us
        our heart to heart melody
        floating through the air

        Colleen Selvon-Rampersad aka cosera

        haibun / haiku

at sunrise
in lotus position
a drop of sweat

Lux

Autumn

moonlight glimmers
a barn owl's shadow
this October night

Maureen Edden

autumn rain
my umbrella stitches
still hold

Srinivasa Rao Sambangi

an Algonquin swears
as his fishpole snaps
sturgeon moon

Colleen Selvon-Rampersad aka cosera

one over-ripe pear
between limbs
in late autumn moonlight
the taste of fall's chill
spurs my thirst for hot cider

Kathryne Ankney Higheagle

citrus orchard
the earthworms and I
diligently digging

Kanjini Devi

cherry crossing
pine cones fall down with
crow's caw

Madhu Singh

apple orchard days summer arrives with spring's demise
a shaded bench scent of blossoms weighs it down
petals scatter through branches the wind moves on

Sue Colpitts

Sijo

shinrin- yoku (forest bathing)

golden canopy
sky drizzles
into upturned hands

leaves floating fall
my shoulders drop

spiny cupules
crunch underfoot
chestnut bulbul's cry

inhale, exhale
pushing up through pine needles
pungent mushrooms

boughs keep bowing
autumn wind

filled with the forest-
peace and ripe berries
I take with me

Anton R. Kelian & Sue Colpitts

autumn breeze
in the katsura tree
a monk's saffron robe

Orense Nicod

half the moon

this garden where we walked today
is dark and rustling 'neath the moon

no matter how many colored flowers
they're painted black by the silver moon

the raat ki rani fragrance scents
the silver rays of this mottled moon

so hard to fall asleep my darling
in the laughing light of this shifting moon

the curtain stirring in the breeze
must have sliced off half the moon

in my restless dreams I know,
I know I sent you half the moon

I kept the other half with me
so we could make a new full moon

but there it is, it's laughing at me
this ugly, dented mocking moon

tell me why...why don't you want it?
all my love and half the moon?

Suraja Roychowdhury

Ghazal

leaves falling one by one
from the old oak tree
a strong gust
thoughts of snow
covering the ground

Diane Allen Hemingway

solo flight
of the fledgling
empty nest
a few remnant feathers
to stroke memories

Ron Russell

twilight --
sparrows squabble
among the rose hips

Gina

a clock
on the mantelpiece
falling leaves

Michael Morris

chick-a-dee - Rengay

the final leaf
of an oak spirals
a toad's smile

a touch of fall
the cat suns

red kite
brushes full moon's face
a tailwind

frolicky pup
I'll have to rake
again

bluegrass in the morning
silvery dew blinks

autumn's
first cold snap
chick-a-dee

Kathryne Ankney Higheagle and James W. McRight Jr.

>   3 line - Katie
>   2 line - James
>   3 line - Katie
>   3 line - James
>   2 line - Katie
>   3 line – James

Winter

how strange
he brings me comfort
that unknown lover
who treads the virgin snow
in a dead poet's verse

Claire Rosilda

snow draped
mountain ranges
Montana - my, my
time to wrap up
in every coat!

Kanjini Devi

winter dusk
between the pines
stare of an owl
comes to the end of the snow
short life of a vole

Sue Colpitts

were you not
in Iceland yesterday?
winter sun

Anton R. Kelian

drifting flakes
I blink away
my last dream

..

frozen
on the driveway
yesterday's news

Suraja Roychowdhury

stacked firewood
the sun worshiping lizard's
temple to Ra

Marlene E. Kasahara

A wave of winter:

It's like the long ride and the question, are we there yet. That scent wave of baking cookies wafts through the house.

are they
done yet

In a little while, I say, but these are not for you. WHAT???!!!

I'll be taking them to the PTA meeting, you know, where we talk about school, homework, kids, the good and the bad of it all.

frowny faces
I open
the oven door

I've been good, he says. Have not, says, she. have to, have not, have to, have not.

dark chocolate chips
in oatmeal
mmm

That's supposed to be good for us. Can I try one. I imagine you can, but you may not.

oh, come on

A little more taunting: I take a cooled cookie in my hand and take a small bite. Perfect, I say.

But, let me be sure. I take another bite, and another, and another.

Let me be the judge of that, he says. May I help, she asks.

Well, I suppose so, you may both help with the cleanup.

WHAT?

Yes, you may both help with the cleanup, after you test the cookies. Take two each, and save the rest for tomorrow.

haibun

Diane Allen Hemingway

winter fog hides the moon
through my window
ghost fingers drift
across my face
the sting of icy words

Maureen Edden

etchings
on the windowpane
another log

Ron Russell

how amazing to see
something flowing
in deep winter
but it is
from the poor woman's eyes

Srinivasa Rao Sambangi

full moon
the last persimmon
drops

Gina

Winter's gone too soon from New Delhi. Like a prisoner let off early from Tihar for good behaviour. This year it even spared the potted plants. Even through chillai kalan or the deep freeze, I didn't once long for it to be summer. Its premature withdrawal has left me wistful; like a lover laments the hurried departure of a paramour. As I box away my woolies, I will count the months till its return.

> bumblebees
> with the first gust
> of spring breeze
> distractedly she
> flicks a curled lock

haibun

Madhu Singh

the taste
of grey air
a shiver

Michael Morris

snow cascaded
as he fell downstream
he was sorry to revive
when Joran kissed him
'it was magical, this snow globe world'

* Joran, the Japanese princess of snow

Colleen Selvon-Rampersad aka *cosera*

traces of snow
as winter seeps bone deep
a cold bench
I feed the one-legged pigeon
despite the sign

Orense Nicod

Lose Yourself, by Eminem

These tanka use one of the lines from the song,
the music the moment.

under the moon
I hold your hand
the music the moment
we are rockets
shooting for the stars

Jason Mackey

wood winds
flurry a fledgling
the music the moment
a trembler first
trusts the buoyant air

Diane Hines

learned in a wood
cougars' blue eyes manifest
the music the moment
chest boomba-booms
till metre decrescendos

Kathryne Ankney Higheagle

golden sunrise
at airport touchdown
the music the moment
will I know this soldier
after his surgery

Colleen Selvon-Rampersad

my steps
quickening
the music the moment
I climb the mountain
reaching the summit

Maureen Edden

like swallows
in summer's fresh rush
the music the moment
when songs of long gone poets
soar away on feathered wings

Madhu Singh

dusk deepens
to strains of live jazz
the music the moment
our eyes meet
across a dance floor

Firdaus Parvez

the time is always right
to make decisions
the music the moment
forward stepping
I hear the tunes

Diane Allen Hemingway

Afterword

We thank AllPoetry.com for opening a site where anyone can become a member to write and read poetry. This is where we all met. Most of us didn't start out writing Oriental poetry, but the site, unknowingly, took us there.

We write mostly haiku and tanka, but also dabble in the other forms you have read in the book. They are forms from the Orient, which we write in English.

This time we chose to do seasons: spring, summer, autumn, winter and the added, Covid, which continues to be in our lives. Also, we added tanka using one of rapper, Eminem's songs, Lose Yourself. The tanka uses, a line from the song, the music the moment, as the line 3 bridge.

Enjoy reading over and over.

Diane Allen Hemingway

www.ingramcontent.com/pod-product-compliance
Lightning Source LLC
Chambersburg PA
CBHW060816050426
42449CB00008B/1684